HEAVEN
FOR KIDS

Ed Strauss

BARBOUR
PUBLISHING

Published by Barbour Publishing, Inc., P.O. Box 719, Uhrichsville, Ohio 44683
www.barbourbooks.com

Our mission is to publish and distribute inspirational products offering exceptional value and biblical encouragement to the masses.

Member of the
Evangelical Christian
Publishers Association

Printed in the United States of America.
Versa Press, East Peoria, IL 61611; October 2013; D10004168

Contents

Introduction

How much do you know about Heaven? Most kids your age don't know much. And that's not really surprising. After all, you haven't been so many years in this world. True, you've already learned a ton of stuff, but you still have so, so much to learn. That's why you spend hours in school every day:

- learning reading and writing
- solving math problems
- discovering amazing science facts
- figuring out where states and cities are
- studying important people and dates in history

And you still have many more years of school to go.

When you think about the future, you most likely don't think about the far-away future when you die and go to Heaven. Instead, you probably think about how you'll do on your next spelling test. Or you wonder what you'll get on your birthday in a few months. Or you imagine what you'll be when you grow up.

So why should you learn about your future, faraway life in Heaven? Well, if someone you know dies, then you need to know about Heaven. Or if you have to bury a pet, you might wonder if it went to Heaven. If your mom or dad tells you, "They're in Heaven now," suddenly you have lots of questions about Heaven, the Kingdom of God: "Where is

Heaven? What is it like? Is it something like this world—or is it completely different? And what do people do there?"

You may have seen cartoons that show people in Heaven:

- standing around on fluffy clouds
- dressed in long, white robes
- with wings on their backs
- with halos over their heads
- playing harps all the time

When you see that, you probably think, *This is a joke, right?* You sure hope that's just someone's imagination, because that's not something you'd enjoy doing for ever and ever. Yes, those are just people's funny ideas. But you'd be surprised how even many adults think this is what Heaven is actually like.

If you've read the Bible, you see that it describes Heaven this way:

- a gigantic city made of gold and jewels
- streets made of pure gold
- people living in beautiful, big houses called mansions
- a River of Life flowing through the city
- fountains and gardens and Trees of Life
- people riding great white horses
- tame lions, leopards, and cobras

Wow! Now, that sounds a lot more exciting and fun than standing on clouds playing harps all day. In fact, it sounds a little bit too fantastic, like something out of a science-fiction movie. Heaven seems so wonderful that some people ask, "Is it just a story? Or is that what God's Kingdom is really like?"

Do you ever wonder about Heaven? Well then, read on, and see what God's Word, the Bible, has to say about that wonderful place.

Chapter 1
What Is Heaven and Where Is It?

If you ask most Christians what Heaven is, they answer that it's the very special, beautiful place where God lives. His Son, Jesus, lives there, too, along with millions of angels. And when Christians die, they go there to live with God and all their saved loved ones. And they'll live there forever. All of these things are true— and this is wonderful news!

Sadly, many people don't know much more about Heaven than this. So they try to imagine what it's like. But if they don't get their facts from the Bible, they end up with some strange ideas. For example, the idea that life in Heaven means standing around on clouds all day strumming harps forever. How boring!

> What does it mean to be saved? Jesus died on the cross to save us from our sins. When people believe in Jesus and what He did, then they are "saved."

The Three Heavens

What is Heaven really? The Bible speaks about three different heavens:

1. "The heavens" means the sky where clouds float and birds fly.
2. "The highest heavens" means outer space where planets and stars are.
3. And "Heaven" is the holy place where God and the angels live.

People today still call the sky "the heavens." And scientists talk about looking through their telescopes "deep into the highest heavens."

Here's a verse that talks about "the heavens" as the sky:

Then God said, "Let the. . .birds fly above the earth across. . .the heavens." GENESIS 1:20 NKJV

And here's one that talks about "the heavens" as outer space:

"You made the heavens, even the highest heavens, and all their starry host." NEHEMIAH 9:6 NIV

Those are the first two heavens. The third Heaven is Paradise, where God lives. One of Jesus' followers, a man named Paul, said:

I was caught up to the third heaven. . . . I was caught up to paradise. 2 CORINTHIANS 12:2, 4 NLT

Jesus in the Clouds

Many people think that Heaven is in the clouds. They get this idea from reading about Jesus' return to Earth someday.

"And they will see the Son of Man coming on the clouds of heaven." MATTHEW 24:30 NLT

After that, we. . .will be caught up together with them. We will be taken up in the clouds. We will meet the Lord in the air. And we will be with him forever. 1 THESSALONIANS 4:17 NIrV

One day, we don't know when, Jesus will come back to Earth. He will appear in the sky where everybody on Earth can see Him. Then people who are alive in that day will be caught up to meet him "in the clouds. . .in the air." But they won't stay there in the air forever. That's not Heaven. That's just where those people will meet Jesus. Once they join Him in the air, *then* Jesus will take them to Heaven.

The time when Jesus returns in the sky to call His believers up to join Him is called "the rapture."

It's kind of like waiting at a bus stop. The bus stop isn't school. You wait at the bus stop for the bus, and when it comes, you get on board and the bus takes you to school.

Bigger Than the Universe

If Heaven isn't in the sky, where *is* it? Is it in outer space, somewhere among the stars? Some people think so. A Bible man named Job asked:

"Isn't God in the highest parts of heaven? See how high the highest stars are!" Job 22:12 NIrv

Job was asking a question. He really wanted to know. King Solomon, the wisest man who ever lived, gave the answer. Solomon built a temple for God. Some of God's people, the Israelites, thought that God would come down to Earth to live in the "house of God." But Solomon knew that

God was far too big to fit inside the temple. Solomon said:

"After all, the heavens can't hold him. In fact, not even the highest heavens can hold him." 2 Chronicles 2:6 NIrV

Did you get that? God is *so* awesome and powerful and big that—

- a great temple can't hold Him
- the heavens (our sky) can't hold Him
- the highest heavens (outer space, the universe) can't hold Him

If God is too big to fit inside our universe, where *does* He live? He lives *outside* of it, in a "high and holy place," in forever (Isaiah 57:15 NKJV). In other words, God lives in Heaven, and Heaven is in a world all its own.

The Heavenly Dimension

A "dimension" is like another world right beside this world, only you can't see it. But sometimes God allows a small opening between the two worlds.

In the story *The Lion, the Witch, and the Wardrobe,* four children were living in an old house in England. But when they walked through the wardrobe (a kind of closet), they came out the other side into a different world called Narnia. Narnia is only a made-up story, but you get the idea. It was a separate world. It was right beside our world, but was "outside" it. That's what the heavenly dimension is

like. Heaven is in a world all by itself, in a place next to our world—but it's a place that we cannot see.

One day, long ago, a prophet named Elisha was in a city called Dothan. An enemy army surrounded the city, and Elisha's young helper was scared. As far as he could see, they were trapped and there was no one to help them.

But Elisha was a very godly man, and the Lord allowed him to see a little way into the heavenly dimension.

"Don't be afraid!" Elisha told him. "For there are more on our side than on theirs!" Then Elisha prayed, "O LORD, open his eyes and let him see!" The LORD opened the young man's eyes, and when he looked up, he saw that the hillside around Elisha was filled with horses and chariots of fire. 2 KINGS 6:16–17 NLT

Can you imagine being able to peek into Heaven and see what's going on there? Elisha had no idea, until God allowed him to see, that a whole army of angels was right there with him and ready to fight the enemy.

God's prophets were special messengers, people whom God trusted to pass His words along to others.

Our Five Senses

Maybe you have learned about the five senses in school:

- sight
- hearing
- taste
- smell
- touch

Most people depend on sight and touch more than the other senses. That's why they say, "Unless I can see something, I won't believe it's there. Unless I can touch it and feel it, I won't believe it's real."

Invisible but Real

Heaven is invisible. It's kind of like the cell phone messages that are in the air all around us, even though we can't see them. We can't touch them. We can't even hear them unless we have a phone ourselves. It picks up the invisible radio waves in the air and changes them into sounds our ears can hear.

It's the same with the wind: Most of the time it's invisible—unless it becomes a tornado. Yet look how powerful the wind is! Over time, it can even erode (wear away) stones.

Here are some things that are invisible, yet they're real:

- air and wind
- X-rays
- smells
- love

The wind has created fantastic sandstone sculptures in states such as Colorado, Arizona, Nevada, and Utah. For example, Delicate Arch is a world-famous stone arch in Arches National Park in Utah. It is 65 feet tall and very beautiful. And the amazing thing is that it was almost totally carved by an invisible force—the wind.

So when people ask, "If God is real, why can't we see Him? Why can't we see Heaven? Where is it?"—the answer is, we can't see them because our human eyes aren't made to see them. Our five senses can only tell us things about *this* world. We can't learn about heavenly things with our senses because they're *outside* our earthly dimension. They are in an invisible world.

That's the reason that we can't see

- God
- Jesus, God's Son
- the holy angels
- our own spirits
- Heaven

Your spirit, also called your soul, is the part of you that is connected to God through your thoughts and feelings.

The Windows of Heaven
In the Bible, God promises to open up "the windows of Heaven."

"I will throw open the windows of heaven. I will pour out so many blessings that you will not have enough room for them." MALACHI 3:10 NIrV

Some people think that these windows are like modern glass windows, and that angels and the people who are in Heaven can look through them and watch us here on Earth. That's *not* what the Bible is talking about. The "windows of Heaven" are like a crevice, a crack in a stone cliff just big enough to squeeze through. The windows of Heaven allow humans to peek from the earthly dimension into the heavenly dimension. Sort of like the wardrobe that the children Peter, Susan, Edmund, and Lucy, from *The Lion, the Witch, and the Wardrobe,* walked through to get from England into Narnia.

A Bible person named Isaiah prayed to God:

I wish you would open up your heavens and come down to us! ISAIAH 64:1 NIrV

Isaiah wanted God to create an opening and come through from the heavenly dimension. And that's exactly what God did at times.

Sometimes, God opened the heavens—the sky we see—and came down to Earth. Other times, God let people like Isaiah simply look through a tiny opening into Heaven itself.

He opened the heavens and came down. PSALM 18:9 NLT

Times Heaven Has Opened

One day, God opened Heaven and let a man named Ezekiel peek into the heavenly dimension:

In my thirtieth year. . . while I was among the exiles by the Kebar River, the heavens were opened and I saw visions of God. Ezekiel 1:1 NIV

This also happened when Jesus was baptized by John in the Jordan River:

After his baptism, as Jesus came up out of the water, the heavens were opened and he saw the Spirit of God descending like a dove and settling on him. Matthew 3:16 NLT

People Who Have Visited Heaven

You might wonder, "If God and angels can come down to Earth, can people go from Earth to Heaven and come back to tell us what they've seen?" The answer is yes. It doesn't happen often, but sometimes it does. In the Bible, Jesus' disciple John wrote:

Then as I looked, I saw a door standing open in heaven, and the same voice I had heard before spoke to me. . . . The voice said, "Come up here, and I will show you what must happen after this." REVELATION 4:1 NLT

John was taken into Heaven. He passed through the open door, and the first thing he saw was God sitting upon His throne in Heaven. In a book of the Bible called Revelation, John wrote about how beautiful and wonderful Heaven is. John also told about the angels and people he saw there.

You may have heard about modern people who have visited Heaven. Often what they describe makes it sound like they really were there. Sometimes, however, people say they have seen Heaven, but what they describe doesn't agree with the Bible. That's why in this book we'll only tell you what God's Word, the Bible, says about Heaven.

In 2003, a four-year-old boy named Colton Burpo said that he was taken to Heaven, where he saw Jesus and spoke with his great-grandpa, who had died before Colton was born. Colton describes what he saw in the book, *Heaven Is for Real.*

Chapter 2
What Is Heaven Like?

Heaven Is Real

Some people have the idea that Heaven is a kind of make-believe place. They can't see or touch it, so they think that it must not be as real as Earth. They imagine that heavenly things are about as solid as a cloud. . .which isn't solid at all, kind of like cotton candy.

Imagine talking to a man who has lived his whole life in a land filled with huts made of sticks and dried mud. You explain to him that the skyscrapers of modern cities are made out of super-strong materials called steel and titanium and cement. These skyscrapers are hundreds of feet high, and covered with glass windows that reflect the sun. What would you think if the man laughed and insisted that buildings are *only* made from sticks and mud? Since he has never heard about or seen steel and titanium and glass, he believes that skyscrapers aren't real.

You would laugh back at him for being so foolish.

Do you know that Heaven is as real as Earth? In fact, it's made out of even stronger materials. God's materials are better than any earthly building blocks because they last forever.

King David made the tiny town of Jerusalem the capital of Israel, and King Solomon built the temple of God there. God visited the temple, but He didn't live there. God's home is in Heaven, which is sometimes called "the heavenly Jerusalem." It's also called "the Jerusalem that is above" (Galatians 4:26 niv).

Something Real?

Some people say that when the Bible describes Heaven it's just a story. It isn't actually describing a real place. They think that the Bible is trying to show people that Heaven is full of perfect things and joy and peace.

Well, let's look at what the Bible says. It says that Heaven is a great city called New Jerusalem, and it

- shines with the beauty of God
- is made out of gold like clear glass
- has streets of pure, see-through gold
- has twelve gates made of pearl
- has a River of Life flowing through the city
- has Trees of Life growing along the river
- has fountains of heavenly water

Are all these things real? Yes! They're absolutely real. We won't be just floating around on clouds feeling joy and peace. We won't be ghosts. We'll have forever bodies in Heaven, and we'll have forever homes to live in there. We'll have solid floors and streets to walk on. If this wasn't true, Jesus would have told us. He said:

"There are many rooms in my Father's house. If this were not true, I would have told you. I am going there to prepare a place for you." JOHN 14:2 NIrV

We can be sure that the places Jesus has gone to prepare for us are real. And they're more fantastic than anything we can imagine.

"No eye has seen, no ear has heard, and no mind has imagined what God has prepared for those who love him." 1 CORINTHIANS 2:9 NLT

What Heaven Is Made Of

Have you heard people say that the streets of Heaven are made of gold? They say that because that's what John saw and wrote about in the book of Revelation.

And the street of the city was pure gold, like transparent glass. REVELATION 21:21 NKJV

The streets of Heaven aren't the only things made of gold. The entire *heavenly city* is made of the same amazing material.

The city itself was made of pure gold, as clear as glass. REVELATION 21:18 GNT

Are the streets of Heaven *actually* made of pure, clear gold? Is the entire city made out of see-through gold? Well, since God Himself lives there, of course everything is beautiful and fantastic! Heaven is made from stuff that makes earthly gold and jewels seem ordinary.

There's another reason that the buildings and the streets are see-through like glass. John wrote:

In the story *The Wizard of Oz,* Dorothy and her friends walked to the Emerald City on a golden-colored "yellow brick road." There are some real "yellow brick roads" in the United States—but the bricks aren't made of gold. They're just ordinary yellow bricks.

The city does not need the sun or the moon to shine on it, for the glory of God gives it light, and the Lamb is its lamp. REVELATION 21:23 NIV

The amazing beauty and love of God and of the Lamb (which is another name for Jesus), fills the city. All of Heaven is lit up with the light of God. It shines through every wall and street and building. Heaven is a city that glows with God's love, like the way warm, wonderful sunlight glows on a perfect summer day.

There are many special names for Jesus, such as "Son of God," "Lord" (meaning "ruler"), and "Messiah" (meaning "anointed one").

The Wall around the City

There is a huge, high wall surrounding the heavenly city. John tells us:

It had a great, high wall with twelve gates, and with twelve angels at the gates. . . . The twelve gates were twelve pearls, each gate made of a single pearl. REVELATION 21:12, 21 NIV

He also tells us exactly how high this wall is:

The angel also measured the wall, and it was 216 feet high. REVELATION 21:17 GNT

The great wall surrounding Heaven is built on foundation stones covered with twelve kinds of precious gemstones (Revelation 21:19–20 NLT).

- The first is jasper.
- The second is sapphire.
- The third is agate.
- The fourth is emerald.
- The fifth is onyx.
- The sixth is carnelian.
- The seventh is chrysolite.
- The eighth is beryl.
- The ninth is topaz.
- The tenth is chrysoprase.
- The eleventh is jacinth.
- The twelfth is amethyst.

You've probably never *heard* of some of these rare precious stones. Most people can't even pronounce some of the names. Yet they're among the most expensive jewels and gemstones on Earth.

If the walls of the city are 216 feet high, those twelve pearly gates must be gigantic! Since pearls grow inside clams, some people must think, "With pearls that big, imagine the size of the clams!" But God can make pearls without clams. And the gates don't have to be round, just because each is made from a single pearl. Remember, God can make anything any shape and size that He wants.

Heaven Is Huge

You may wonder, "If billions and billions of Christians who have died from all around the world—from all the ages until now—live inside the heavenly city, the city has to be huge! There's no city on Earth big enough to hold *that* many people!" That's true. But Heaven is a different kind of place. And the heavenly city is indeed bigger then anything that exists on Earth.

John said:

The angel who talked to me held in his hand a gold measuring stick to measure the city, its gates, and its wall. When he measured it, he found it was a square, as wide as it was long. In fact, its length and width and height were each 1,400 miles. REVELATION 21:15–16 NLT

Can you wrap your mind around *that*? God's heavenly city, called New Jerusalem, is:

- 1,400 miles long on all sides
- 1,400 miles wide on all sides
- 1,400 miles high on all sides

If you did some math, you would see that if the city were made out of many, many, many cubes (blocks)—and each of those cubes was one mile high, one mile wide, and one mile long—there would be 2,744,000,000 mile-high cubes in the city. That's 2 billion, 744 million blocks of huge living space. Even if you can't do the math—there's lots of room in Heaven!

Heavenly Mansions

One of the best-known promises Jesus made is about our homes in Heaven. He said:

"In My Father's house are many mansions." John 14:2 NKJV

Some people who believe in God dream of these heavenly houses as huge, gorgeous palaces of white stone, with—

- staircases made of gold
- gardens of fruit trees, flowers, and fountains
- gigantic swimming pools
- tame lions, tigers, deer, and peacocks
- angels for servants

Will we have huge houses called *mansions* in Heaven? We don't know for sure, but we'll definitely have wonderful places to live in. They might not be palaces surrounded by huge gardens. Instead, they might be rooms in God's big city-sized mansion. Some people who know a lot about the Bible say Jesus actually meant this in John 14:2:

"There are many rooms in my Father's house." JOHN 14:2 NIRV

The Taj Mahal is one of the most beautiful buildings on Earth. It's a masterpiece made of costly white stone, and took twenty years to build. It looks like a palace, but it's really a gigantic tomb—a burial place—for a wife of the rich ruler who built it. Our homes in Heaven will be even more wonderful than this.

This gives us a hint that we might be living in one humongous city-sized palace—along with lots of other people. And who knows how large and fantastic the rooms will be!

One thing we know for sure: Jesus is preparing a wonderful home for us in His forever place—Heaven. He said:

"I am going there to prepare a place for you. If I go and do that, I will come back. And I will take you to be with me. Then you will also be where I am." John 14:2–3 NIrV

Paradise: Trees and Gardens

God created people to live in Paradise—Heaven! That's why He placed the first human beings, Adam and Eve, in a heaven-like place on Earth called the Garden of Eden. It was also called "Eden, the garden of God" (Ezekiel 28:13 NIV).

In ancient times, people built walls around their gardens to protect them. Our English word, *paradise*, comes from an old word that means "walled garden." God's city in Heaven, New Jerusalem, is surrounded by a high wall and is the best paradise of all.

Most people are excited about living in a shining city made of pure gold, but they don't want *only* buildings, houses, and streets in Heaven. They want to be surrounded by nature.

In Bible times, a "paradise" meant a royal park full of

- unusual and beautiful flower gardens
- fruit trees and nut trees
- lovely, shady walking paths
- fish ponds, streams, and fountains
- peacocks, songbirds, and butterflies
- graceful deer
- magnificent horses

So, we might expect all these things and much more in Heaven.

The Bible says that Heaven is Paradise. When God's Son, Jesus, was dying on the cross, He told the man beside Him:

"Truly I tell you, today you will be with me in paradise."
LUKE 23:43 NIV

One of Jesus' followers named Paul was given a short glimpse of Heaven, too. And he called it Paradise:

But I do know that I was caught up to paradise and heard things so astounding that they cannot be expressed in words. 2 CORINTHIANS 12:3–4 NLT

The most fantastic tree in the earthly Garden of Eden was the Tree of Life. And this tree is right now growing in Heaven, along the banks of the River of Life. If you believe in Jesus, when you get to Heaven you'll be allowed to eat its fruit. John wrote about it in the book of Revelation:

On each side of the river was the tree of life, which bears fruit twelve times a year, once each month. REVELATION 22:2 GNT

"To the one who is victorious, I will give the right to eat from the tree of life, which is in the paradise of God." REVELATION 2:7 NIV

Rivers and Fountains

Heaven's city, New Jerusalem, is full of trees and parks and gardens, and it also has fountains and springs, ponds, rivers and streams. The greatest river in Heaven is the River of Life. John wrote:

Then the angel showed me the river of the water of life, as clear as crystal, flowing from the throne of God and of the Lamb. REVELATION 22:1 NIV

When Christians get to Heaven, Jesus "will shepherd (gather) them and lead them to living fountains of waters. And God will wipe away every tear from their eyes" (Revelation 7:17 NKJV). Notice that it says Jesus will "lead" people to these fountains. We can't find them by ourselves. Maybe they're in secret gardens in Heaven. One thing we do know for sure: Jesus will lead to us to them.

Here on Earth, our bodies need water to live. Without water, we would die in a few days. In Heaven, we will have "living water" as Jesus promised: "Anyone who is thirsty may drink from the spring of the water of life" (Revelation 21:6 NIrV).

God's heavenly water is there for everyone. Some of the last, beautiful words in the Bible say:

"Let anyone who is thirsty come. Let anyone who desires drink freely from the water of life." REVELATION 22:17 NLT

Chapter 3
Who Is in Heaven
Now?

God the Father

Our forever God, the Creator of the heavens and the Earth, also created Heaven. And He created the heavenly city called New Jerusalem as its capital. So of course *He* lives there. In fact, God is the very center of Heaven. All the angels gather in front of His throne to worship Him.

Now, here's a mystery: the Bible tells us that

- God is invisible (1 Timothy 1:17).
- God lives in such a bright light that no one can get close to Him (1 Timothy 6:16).
- No one has seen God. No one can see Him (1 Timothy 6:16).

You may wonder, then, "If no one can get close to God, if He's invisible and no one can see Him, then why did some people have visions—meaning, to see with heavenly eyes—God sitting upon a throne?"

The answer is simple: our earthly senses weren't made to see God's heavenly world. So we can't see God with our human eyes. But sometimes God has allowed people to peek into Heaven and see God with the new eyes they will have when they get there.

Jesus said, "Blessed are the pure in heart, for they shall see God" (Matthew 5:8 nkjv). We can't see God *now* with our human eyes, but one day in Heaven we *will* see God in all His beauty and glory.

When Ezekiel had his vision of God (see Ezekiel 1:26–28 NIrV), he saw God sitting on a throne that looked like it was made of sapphire—a gorgeous blue gemstone.

- On the throne. . .was a figure that appeared to be human.
- From his waist up he looked like glowing metal that was full of fire.
- From his waist down he looked like fire.
- Bright light surrounded him.
- The glow around him looked like a rainbow in the clouds on a rainy day.

A Bible man named Daniel also had a vision of God on His throne (Daniel 7:9–10 NIrV). Daniel described how God looked:

- His clothes were as white as snow.
- The hair on his head was white like wool.
- His throne was blazing with fire.
- Flames were all around its wheels.
- A river of fire was flowing. . .in front of God.
- Thousands and thousands of angels served him.

John saw God's throne in Heaven, too, he wrote:

I saw a throne in heaven and someone sitting on it. The one sitting on the throne was as brilliant as gemstones—like jasper and carnelian. And the glow of an emerald circled his throne like a rainbow. Twenty-four thrones surrounded him, and twenty-four elders sat on them. . . . From the throne came flashes of lightning and the rumble of thunder. REVELATION 4:2–5 NLT

John said that God reminded him of expensive jewel stones called jasper and carnelian. Jasper means "spotted or speckled stone," and it's usually a rich red color. But jasper can also be yellow, brown, green, or even blue. Carnelian is a reddish-brown stone.

Jesus, the Son of God

When Jesus was on Earth, He had a human body just like us. After He was crucified—that means He died after being nailed on the cross—Jesus came back to life. His human body had died. But then God changed it into a forever body that could never die again. Many people saw Jesus when He came back to life. The Bible says:

After the Lord Jesus had talked with them, he was taken up to heaven and sat at the right side of God.
MARK 16:19 GNT

After being on Earth for a while, Jesus went up to Heaven to be with His Father, God.

Jesus tells us that the right hand of the throne of God is *part* of God's throne. He said, "I also overcame and sat down with My Father on His throne" (Revelation 3:21 NKJV). Jesus is worthy to sit on God's throne with Him because Jesus *is* God. This is why Christians not only worship God the Father, but Jesus, God the Son.

Jesus' forever body still has the wounds from the nails in His hands and feet. And He still has the spear wound in His side where a soldier stabbed Him while He was nailed to the cross. God could have taken away those wounds when He gave Jesus His new body, but God wanted people to always remember that Jesus died so they also could live in Heaven someday.

Even though Jesus is now in Heaven, He still looks like a man. When His disciples—His followers—saw Him after He came back from being dead, Jesus looked perfectly human. Many people since then have had visions of Jesus. They say that He looks like a man—only He glows with light. They saw Jesus only in *part* of His glory. Someday in Heaven, Christians will see Jesus Christ in His *full* glory. John said,

But we know that when Christ appears. . .we shall see him as he is. 1 John 3:2 NIV

The word *glory* means "amazing beauty and brightness." Something "glorious" is almost too beautiful for words. Have you ever seen something glorious?

Jesus is part of God and has "the brightness of his glory" (Hebrews 1:3 KJV). This is how John described Jesus (Revelation 1:13–16 GNT):

- He was wearing a robe that reached to His feet.
- He had a gold band around His chest.
- His hair was white as snow.
- His eyes blazed like fire.
- His feet shone like polished brass.
- His voice sounded like a roaring waterfall.
- His face was as bright as the midday sun.

Jesus sits in a glorious throne at the right hand of His Father, ruling over Heaven forever. Strange beings called "cherubim" and twenty-four elders (very important men) sit near the throne and praise God and Jesus both. And all the angels around God's throne also worship Jesus, the Son of God.

Cherubim—Fearsome Beasts

Normally, when people think of who's in Heaven, they forget about the strange creatures called the *zoon*. Have you never heard of the zoon? It's an old-time word from the country of Greece, and since John wrote in Greek, that's what he called them. In one old version of the Bible, they're called *beasts*:

In the midst of the throne, and round about the throne, were four beasts full of eyes before and behind.
REVELATION 4:6 KJV

Some people who rewrote the Bible in words we can more easily understand thought that "beasts" sounded too much like "monsters." So they called the zoon "living creatures." Ezekiel tells us what these "living creatures" look like:

I saw what looked like four living creatures in human form, but each of them had four faces and four wings. Their legs were straight, and they had hoofs like those of a bull. They shone like polished bronze. In addition to their four faces and four wings, they each had four human hands, one under each wing. EZEKIEL 1:5–8 GNT

Wow! Can you imagine that?

And what do the four faces look like on these living creatures? Ezekiel 1:10 (GNT) tells us:

a human face

a lion's face

a bull's face

an eagle's face

Later, Ezekiel called these creatures *cherubim* (Ezekiel 10:1). One of the creatures is called a "cherub," and more than one are called "cherubim."

Many people think of a *cherub* as a chubby baby angel, often shooting a tiny bow and arrow like an imaginary Cupid. That's not what a cherub is at all! It's a magnificent, mysterious, somewhat scary-looking creature.

Seraphim—the Burning Ones

You'll be surprised to learn that there are even more creatures in Heaven! *Seraphim* are mentioned very little in the Bible. But don't worry: Seraphim are in no danger of going away. They're powerful, holy, forever beings. Nobody can touch them!

In Hebrew, one of the languages the Bible was written in, *seraphim* means "the burning ones." No one is sure why they have this name. Maybe they're white-hot from being so close to God's light. Maybe it's because of what they do. Isaiah said, when he told about his visit to Heaven: "Then one of the seraphim flew to me with a burning coal he had taken from the altar" (Isaiah 6:6 NLT).

We know almost nothing about seraphim except for what it says in Isaiah 6:1–3, 6 (NIV):

- Seraphim have six wings.
- They cover their faces with two wings.
- They cover their feet with two wings.
- They fly with two wings.
- They have human hands.
- They apparently have human bodies.

The Amazing Angels

Some people believe that when humans die, they become angels. But that's not true. Angels are different beings. God made the angels before He created humans. One day we'll have glorious bodies and powers *like* angels, but we won't *become* angels. In Revelation 7, John writes about a great crowd of people (in verse 9), then describes a crowd of angels (in verse 11).

The Bible doesn't tell us how many angels there are, but one Bible verse tells us that millions of angels gathered around God's throne (Daniel 7:10). And another verse says that there is "an innumerable company of angels" in the heavenly Jerusalem (Hebrews 12:22 NKJV). "An innumerable company of angels" means there were so many angels that no one could count them all.

So what exactly *are* angels?

- They're glorious heavenly beings.
- They're more powerful than humans.
- Their name means "messenger," so they're God's messengers.
- They enjoy worshipping God and singing.
- They can always see God.
- They watch over and protect humans.
- They celebrate when humans are saved from sin.
- They're wise but don't know everything.

There is a special class of ruling angels called archangels (1 Thessalonians 4:16). Archangel means chief angel. "Michael, the great prince. . . one of the chief princes" is one of these archangels (Daniel 12:1; 10:13 niv).

God sends His angels to serve and protect us:

All angels are spirits who serve. God sends them to serve those who will receive salvation. HEBREWS 1:14 NIrV

God will put his angels in charge of you to protect you wherever you go. PSALM 91:11 GNT

Regular angels are powerful, but archangels are so magnificent and glorious that they look out-of-this-world.

We often picture angels with two wings, but the Bible never says angels have wings. The only heavenly beings with wings are cherubim (four wings each) and seraphim (six wings each). And they're not angels. They're one-of-a-kind, special creatures.

Daniel once saw the archangel Gabriel (Daniel 10:5–6 GNT), and Daniel described him like this:

- He was wearing linen clothes and a belt of fine gold.
- His body shone like a jewel.
- His face was as bright as a flash of lightning.
- His eyes blazed like fire.
- His arms and legs shone like polished bronze.
- His voice sounded like the roar of a great crowd.

Saved People

When our saved loved ones die, angels take their spirits to Heaven to be with God and Jesus. As soon as they leave this world, they are "present with the Lord" (2 Corinthians 5:8 NKJV). Jesus' follower Paul was excited about going to Heaven. He said:

For to me, living means living for Christ, and dying is even better. . . . I'm torn between two desires: I long to go and be with Christ, which would be far better for me. PHILIPPIANS 1:21, 23 NLT

For the past 2,000 years, ever since Jesus died on the cross to save us, Christians have been going to Heaven when they die. There are now millions upon millions of Christians there. And they come from all over the Earth. When John was visiting Heaven, he saw "a vast (huge) crowd, too great to count. . .standing in front of the throne"

(Revelation 7:9 NLT). They were from —

- every nation
- every tribe
- every people
- every language

If someone you know has died, and they believed in Jesus, they're in Heaven right now. They're enjoying Paradise with millions of other Christians. They aren't old, tired, sick, or hurt anymore. They're never sad anymore. They're now in the most beautiful place ever. And if you believe in Jesus, you'll see them again one day—and be with them forever.

When people who love Jesus die, they aren't called "dead Christians." Instead, they're sometimes called "departed believers," because they've believed in Jesus and departed (left) this life to go to be with Him in Heaven. Their human bodies are dead, but their spirits are very much alive!

Chapter 4
What Will We Do in Heaven?

Praising God and Playing Harps

John saw a great crowd of people in Heaven, and they were holding palm branches in their hands, and worshipping and praising God (Revelation 7:9–10). Then John heard a sound "like the music of harps being played." John later saw people who "held harps given to them by God" (Revelation 14:2; 15:2 NIrV).

> To "praise" someone is to say good things about him or her. People praise God by saying (or singing) how good He is, how powerful He is, and how special He is.

When some people read these things that John wrote, they get the idea that all they'll *ever* do in Heaven is strum on harps, wave palm branches, and praise God. Many Christians would enjoy that for a while, but wouldn't like to do *only* that forever. Even people who like harp music wouldn't want to listen to it all the time.

These gatherings around God's throne are probably special occasions. We won't gather in huge crowds like that all the time. The heavenly city, New Jerusalem, is a very big place, and it's full of many other interesting, exciting, and fun things to do.

When we see God face-to-face in Heaven, we won't find it boring to praise Him. God is incredibly beautiful and filled with love, and worshipping Him will give us great happiness. It will be our highest joy in Heaven. We'll probably have a hard time pulling our eyes away from Him.

Meeting Our Loved Ones

One of the best things about Heaven is that we'll be to-gether again with our family members and friends who have died. We were sad when they died, but when we see them in Heaven we'll never have to say "good-bye" again. Imagine walking through the gardens of Paradise with your great-great-grandfather! Think of all the amazing stories he could tell you.

Many people believe that when they arrive in Heaven, the first people to greet them will be their loved ones. But how will our loved ones know that we're coming? Well, the angels know a lot about us here on Earth:

- They know what we're doing and guard us (Psalm 91:11).
- They know when we believe and are saved (Luke 15:10).
- They know when we die, and they bring us to Paradise (Luke 16:22).

Since the angels know exactly when we're coming to Heaven, for sure they'll tell our loved ones who live there. Our family members and friends in Heaven love us and care about us, so they'll be there to greet us when we get there.

Spending Time with Bible Heroes

When you get to Heaven you might also spend time talking with great men and women of the Bible. You could—

- ask Noah how he built such a huge ship and if all those animals got along together
- ask Moses what it was like to split the sea wide open so people could walk through it
- ask Joshua what it sounded like when the walls of Jericho fell down
- ask Joseph how it felt to be picked on by his brothers and then, later, rule over all of Egypt
- ask David if he felt afraid to fight the scary giant, Goliath
- ask Peter how it felt when he walked on water

Will we get the chance to talk with heroes from the Bible? Jesus said:

"I say to you that many will come from east and west, and sit down with Abraham, Isaac, and Jacob (people from the Bible) in the kingdom of heaven." MATTHEW 8:11 NKJV

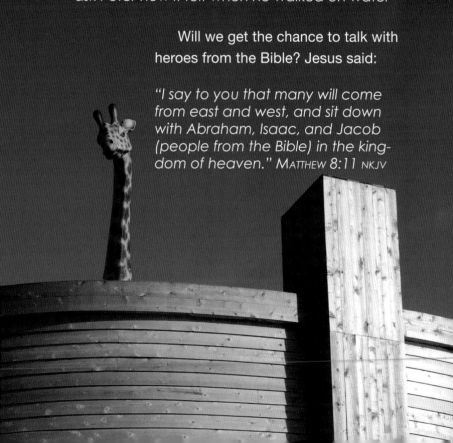

Eating and Drinking in Heaven

Will we eat and drink in Heaven? The main reason we eat and drink on Earth is to keep our human bodies alive. But in Heaven we'll have our forever bodies. So maybe we won't *need* to eat. But we'll still want to have parties with others and taste delicious food.

When we eat in the kingdom of Heaven, we most likely will sit down to enjoy a great feast. The Bible says:

"I say to you that many will come from the east and the west, and will take their places at the feast with Abraham, Isaac and Jacob in the kingdom of heaven."
MATTHEW 8:11 NIV

The Bible says that long ago a king named Xerxes made a great banquet here on Earth. He didn't just serve delicious food, but he made the feast as special as possible (Esther 1:3–7 GNT).

- The banquet lasted a whole week.
- It was held in the gardens of the royal palace.
- The courtyard was decorated with blue and white curtains.
- The curtains were tied by purple cords to silver rings on marble columns.
- The courts were made of white marble, shining mother-of-pearl, and blue turquoise.
- Couches made of gold and silver were placed in the courts.
- Drinks were served to guests in gold cups.

Xerxes was just an earthly king—yet he held a wonderful feast to make his guests happy. Imagine how much more fantastic God's feasts will be in Heaven!

Through an angel, God told John: "Happy are those who have been invited to the wedding feast of the Lamb" (Revelation 19:9 GNT). If you believe in Jesus, you're definitely invited to this special feast in Heaven, and your name will be called when it's time to enjoy this greatest of all banquets!

What Will We Eat?

What kind of food will we feast on in Heaven? Jesus promises, "To him who overcomes I will give some of the hidden manna to eat" (Revelation 2:17 NKJV).

When some of God's people were wandering in the desert for forty years, God "opened the doors of heaven" and did something amazing. He allowed a strange food that looked like flakes to rain down on the hungry people so they would always have something to eat. God "gave them bread from heaven" called *manna*. The people "ate the food of angels!" (see Psalm 78:23–25 NLT).

Manna was amazing stuff, but the food in Heaven is not *ordinary* manna. Jesus called it *"hidden* manna." Think about it like this: When you're having guests and your mom buys a mouth-watering dessert, she hides it so that you don't eat it all before dinner. But wow! When it's time for dessert, it's worth the wait. This hidden manna will be like that—extra-delicious.

God also promises that you'll eat the fruit of the Tree of Life (Revelation 2:7). God wouldn't even let Adam and Eve eat it. In fact, they had to leave the Garden of Eden to make *sure* they didn't sneak a bite. But *you'll* get to eat it when you get to Heaven.

And that's just *some* of what's on the menu. Jesus ate different kinds of food after He came back from being dead and was in His forever body. He ate a piece of fish and some honeycomb (Luke 24:41–43 NKJV). And His disciple Peter said that the disciples "ate and drank" with Jesus after He came back to life (Acts 10:41 NKJV).

So we'll be eating lots of different food:

- We'll eat yummy new foods we never knew existed.
- We'll eat healthy food that's good for us and won't taste awful.
- There won't be any junk food—but the fast food will be delicious.
- No one will have food allergies anymore.
- No one will ever go hungry.

Animals in Heaven

What else will we do in Heaven? Well, what do you enjoy doing on Earth *now*? Many people like walking with their dogs along shady paths through parks. And since Heaven is the perfect Paradise, romping with their beloved dogs across green lawns, past trees and fountains, would make Heaven *truly* heavenly.

Other things animal lovers would enjoy:

- riding a horse through vast fields of flowers
- petting tame lions and play-wrestling with tigers
- flying with flocks of snow-white swans
- swimming underwater with colorful tropical fish
- water-skiing with dolphins

Many people believe that their pets go to Heaven when they die.

When Jesus is ruling Earth someday (Isaiah 11:1–9) there will be animals around, such as

- wolves
- bears
- leopards
- lions

- sheep and lambs
- goats and kids
- cattle and calves
- snakes

Jesus will rule Earth for a thousand years, and then God will create a brand-new Earth. His heavenly city will move from Heaven to the new Earth then (Revelation 21:1–3). And there will still be animals around! God told Isaiah,

"Look! I am creating new heavens and a new earth, and no one will even think about the old ones anymore. . . . The wolf and the lamb will feed together. The lion will eat hay like a cow. But the snakes will eat dust. In those days no one will be hurt or destroyed on my holy mountain." ISAIAH 65:17, 25 NLT

Learning Forever

There is so, so much that we don't know, and we'll never stop learning in Heaven. You won't have to sit in school and study boring things. You'll study things that you're interested in, and enjoy learning about. You'll be doing lots of exciting jobs that you never did before, and will need to learn how to do them.

You'll be able to ask the great saints of God all your questions—and finally get answers. Angels will be your teachers. Angels have been asking God questions for a long time. They've learned a lot! That's why, all through the Bible, angels have been explaining things to people. Daniel said that when he visited Heaven he heard a voice there ask the angel Gabriel to explain what something meant:

I heard a voice call out over the Ulai River, "Gabriel, explain to him the meaning of what he saw." DANIEL 8:16 GNT

The famous preacher Billy Graham said, "God will prepare everything for our perfect happiness in Heaven, and if it takes my dog being there, I believe he'll be there." Dogs aren't mentioned by name, but if even *wolves* are in Heaven, dogs will be, too. Also, we know there are herds of horses in Heaven (Revelation 19:11, 14). Our pets might just be there, too.

Jobs in Eternity

The world is changing so fast. When you grow up you probably won't have the same job as grownups have today. Your job maybe hasn't been invented yet. Since God's Heaven is *much* greater than our human world, we can't begin to imagine some of the jobs we'll have there. The Bible does give us hints, though.

Some Christians "will rule as kings forever and ever" (Revelation 22:5 GNT). There will be nations and cities and towns and villages all over the Earth. So, God's Kingdom will need —

- kings and queens to rule over nations
- governors to rule provinces and states
- mayors to govern cities and towns and villages
- wise men and women to advise the rulers

John also tells us that when the heavenly city moves to the Earth,

The peoples of the world will walk by its light, and the kings of the earth will bring their wealth into it. . . . The greatness and the wealth of the nations will be brought into the city. REVELATION 21:24–26 GNT

What is the "wealth of the nations" that all the kings of the Earth will bring into this new city? Most likely it will be things like

- gold, silver, and precious metals
- diamonds, rubies, and other gems

- nuts, fruits, and vegetables
- wheat, oats, and rice
- food for animals

And you know what *that* means! Someone will have to mine the gold and silver, and jewels and gems—and others will create beautiful things out of them. And some people will be farmers to grow all the food.

Do you want to be a doctor or a nurse? The Tree of Life grows in Heaven and "its leaves are for the healing of the nations" (Revelation 22:2 GNT). Someone will have to gather those amazing leaves and use them to heal. Maybe it will be you!

Exploring New Worlds

After you do everything you could ever imagine doing on this Earth, maybe you'll look for *new* worlds to explore. Perhaps God will encourage His people to explore new worlds within the galaxy. It would take quite some time to explore the entire Milky Way.

Recently, scientists discovered that our sun is not the only star with planets. They've found hundreds of planets orbiting nearby stars. Our galaxy has some 50 billion

planets, and 500 million can possibly support life. And that's not all. There are about 170 billion galaxies in the universe. We'll never run out of things to do and see.

There will be lots of jobs in the Kingdom of God. Maybe you'll do one job for a hundred years—then when you want to change, do something else for another hundred years, and so on.

Chapter 5
How Do I Get to Heaven?

Paradise: The Garden of Eden

God created human beings to live in Paradise. That's why He put the first people, Adam and Eve, in the Garden of Eden. The garden was perfect like the real Paradise, Heaven. It was also called "Eden, the garden of God" (Ezekiel 28:13 NIV). This garden was filled with beautiful trees loaded with delicious fruit. It also had lots of tame animals. God put two special trees in the garden:

In the middle of the garden he placed the tree of life and the tree of the knowledge of good and evil. GENESIS 2:9 NLT

God told Adam and Eve that they were free to eat the fruit of *almost* any tree. That means they could have eaten

- apples from apple trees
- pears from pear trees
- oranges from orange trees
- cherries from cherry trees
- figs from fig trees
- fruit from the Tree of Life

The only tree that the Lord commanded them *not* to touch was the Tree of the Knowledge of Good and Evil. He told Adam and Eve that if they ate that fruit, they'd die. Adam and Eve obeyed God for a while. But then the Serpent (who was really the Devil) lied to them and talked them into disobeying God by eating the fruit.

Because Adam and Eve sinned, their spirits—the

invisible part within them that connected them with God—died. They were no longer close to God. Also, their human bodies began to grow old and die. If Adam and Eve had eaten the fruit of the Tree of Life, their bodies would have lived forever, but their spirits would have been dark and sinful. So God sent them out of His beautiful garden so they couldn't eat from the Tree of Life.

A famous preacher named Charles Spurgeon wrote, "Sin has shut us out of Eden; yet let us not weep, for Christ has prepared a better Paradise for us in Heaven. God has provided for us 'a pure river of water of life' and a lovelier garden than Eden ever was."

Are You Going to Heaven?

After reading about Heaven and learning what a wonderful place it is, you're probably looking forward to going there one day. But how can you be *sure* that you'll be there? This is a very important question, and you *need* to know the answer to it. You can't just wish or hope that you're good enough, and that God will allow you to enter.

This might surprise you, but none of us are good enough to have forever life with God in Heaven. We've all sinned and disobeyed Him. We've all done wrong, selfish things. Even thinking bad thoughts is a sin. Here are some other sins:

- being selfish with your things
- being disrespectful to parents
- hating someone
- not forgiving others
- doing things to hurt others
- telling a lie
- gossiping about others
- envying others or wanting their things
- stealing—taking other people's things

The Bible says:

Everyone has sinned. No one measures up to God's glory. ROMANS 3:23 NIrV

When you sin, the pay you get is death. ROMANS 6:23 NIrV

If that were all that the Bible said about sin, it would be a very sad story. Since we all sin, all of us deserve to die—which means being apart from God forever. But there's more! The main message of the part of the Bible called the New Testament is the Gospel—and *Gospel* means "good news."

The first part of this next verse tells bad news. But then it tells very, very good news:

When you sin, the pay you get is death. But God gives you the gift of eternal (forever) life because of what Christ Jesus our Lord has done. ROMANS 6:23 NIrV

God would *love* to give you forever life! It would make Him very happy! Jesus said, "So don't be afraid, little flock. For it gives your Father great happiness to give you the Kingdom" (Luke 12:32 NLT).

And *what* did Jesus Christ do for you, and for all of us? He died on the cross for our sins. He saved us from being apart from God. He fixed it so we can enjoy forever life with Him in Heaven.

The Way to Heaven

Many years ago, a man named Billy Sunday visited Pittsburgh, Pennsylvania. He had to go to the post office, so he asked a young boy for directions. As the boy was showing him the way, Billy told the boy that he was going to preach a sermon that evening called, "The Way to Heaven." Billy said that if he'd come to the meeting, the boy could learn how to get to Heaven. But the boy asked, "What? You're going to show me the way to Heaven when you don't even know the way to the post office?"

This is a funny story, but it shows what many people think—that Heaven is so far away and mysterious that it must be hard to figure out how to get there.

But the way to Heaven isn't that hard to find! Jesus said:

"I am the way and the truth and the life. No one comes to the Father except through me." JOHN 14:6 NIV

To have forever life in Heaven, you must

- believe that, just like everyone else, you sin
- understand that you can't earn your way to Heaven by doing good things
- know that you need Jesus to save you from being apart from God forever
- believe that Jesus died on the cross to take the punishment for your sins
- believe that Jesus rose again from the dead
- tell God you're sorry
- ask Jesus to come into your life and be your Lord
- try your best to obey Him

If you do this, you'll be connected with God forever. Some people call this being "born again." It means that God will live inside your heart forever, and you'll become a son or daughter to Him.

God Has Adopted Us

Yes! You can become a son or daughter of God. In the Bible, God says:

I will be your father, and you shall be my sons and daughters. 2 CORINTHIANS 6:18 GNT

You become God's child when you trust His Son, Jesus.

They believed in his name. He gave them the right to become children of God. JOHN 1:12 NIrV

When we are adopted into God's family,
God sends a Helper to live in our hearts. This Helper
is called "the Holy Spirit." The Holy Spirit is the part
of God that helps us to do what is right and to follow
God's plan for our lives.

Being God's child does not mean that your parents here on Earth stop being your mom and dad. But when God adopts us as His own, He becomes our wonderful, amazing, perfect heavenly Father. All who believe and are saved, even grown-ups, become God's children, and He sends His Spirit into their hearts.

Instead, you received God's Spirit when he adopted you as his own children. ROMANS 8:15 NLT

The Bible tells us that all things that belong to God will also belong to us. Jesus said:

"All things that the Father has are Mine." JOHN 16:15 NKJV

That means that God gives to Jesus everything He has. God is so very rich that He wants to share all that He has with His children. It's not surprising that Jesus was given everything in Heaven. But we are *also* heirs of God (Galatians 4:7).

And since we are his children, we are his heirs. In fact, together with Christ we are heirs of God's glory. ROMANS 8:17 NLT

When God says that someone is His "heir," it means that everything He owns also belongs to that person. You are God's child, and Jesus promises to share everything in all of Heaven with you! That's what the Bible means when it says that we've been adopted with "all the rights children have" (Galatians 4:5 NIRV). God will give us all the riches of Heaven!

The Book of Life

John had more to say in the book of Revelation. He wrote:

Only those whose names are written in the Lamb's Book of Life will enter the city. REVELATION 21:27 NIrV

"The Lamb" is another of God's names for Jesus. The moment you ask Jesus to save you, He comes into your life and connects you with God. When that happens, you become God's child forever. There is a book in Heaven called "the Book of Life." When your name gets written in it you become a citizen of the Kingdom of Heaven. When you do die, you'll go straight to Paradise. This is reason to be very happy! Jesus said, "rejoice that your names are written in heaven" (Luke 10:20 NIV).

Jesus said, "I will never erase their names from the Book of Life, but I will announce before my Father and his angels that they are mine" (Revelation 3:5 NLT).

Citizens of Heaven

When God adopts you as His son or daughter, you become a member of His family. You become a citizen of Heaven, and someday Heaven will be your forever home. It doesn't matter where you live now on Earth. When your human body dies, you will get your forever body and go straight to Heaven. You will feel wonderful because Heaven will seem like home to you. You won't feel like a stranger or an outsider there.

So you are no longer strangers and outsiders. You are citizens together with God's people. You are members of God's family. EPHESIANS 2:19 NIrV

"We. . .are citizens of heaven, and we eagerly wait for our Savior, the Lord Jesus Christ, to come from heaven" (Philippians 3:20 GNT).

Forever Life Is a Gift of God

God is our loving heavenly Father. He wants us to live forever in Heaven with Him. And since He knows that we can never do enough good things to earn forever life, He offers it as a gift. The Bible says:

God's grace has saved you because of your faith in Christ. Your salvation doesn't come from anything you do. It is God's gift. It is not based on anything you have done. No one can brag about earning it. EPHESIANS 2:8–9 NIrV

"God's grace has saved you." But what is *grace*? When we thank God for the food we eat, it's called "saying grace." But that's not what *grace* means here. Grace is when someone is very, very kind and generous to you when you don't deserve it. When someone is "gracious," they are kind and forgiving.

Long ago, kings and queens had great power. When people did something wrong and deserved to be punished, they hoped the rulers would be *gracious* when they judged. So when people talked to kings and queens, they called them "your Grace."

Headed to a Heavenly Country

We should enjoy life down here on Earth, but our human bodies won't live forever. Isn't it wonderful to know that someday we'll have new bodies that *will* live forever in Heaven?

Heaven is much better than any country, or any place

at all, here on Earth. So we should look forward to our home in Heaven more than anything that we look forward to on Earth.

Instead, it was a better country they longed for, the heavenly country. And so God is not ashamed for them to call him their God, because he has prepared a city for them. HEBREWS 11:16 GNT

God has a city waiting for us in Heaven. It's "the Holy City, the New Jerusalem" (Revelation 21:2 NIV). We'll live in Heaven forever. That's why Jesus said in Matthew 6:19–21:

- Do not put away riches for yourselves on earth.
- Moths and rust can destroy them.
- Thieves can break in and steal them.
- Instead, obey God and look forward to Heaven.
- There, moths and rust do not destroy anything.
- There, thieves do not break in and steal things.
- Your heart will be with God, where it belongs.

Chapter 6
What Are Heaven's "Rewards"?

Heavenly Rewards

Forever life is not a reward we receive for living a life that pleases God. Forever life is absolutely free! And what a fantastic gift it is! We will

- live forever in a perfect Paradise
- be with our loved ones forever
- eat the fruit of the Tree of Life
- drink living water from fountains
- eat delicious heavenly food

Some people think that because forever life is free, it doesn't matter *how* they live. They'll still go to Heaven even if they don't pray, live selfishly, and disobey God. (After all, obeying God and loving others can be tough sometimes!) So they ask, "Why should I obey God if I get to enjoy all the riches of Heaven anyway?"

The answer is simple: we obey God because we *love* Him. And we love Him because of the great gift of salvation He's given us.

We also obey God because He's promised to reward us if we do. Jesus said:

"Look, I am coming soon! My reward is with me, and I will give to each person according to what they have done." REVELATION 22:12 NIV

Salvation is the "forever life" God gives us when we believe in His Son, Jesus. And the forever life doesn't start in Heaven—we can begin enjoying it right here on Earth!

Some Christians won't have as many treasures in Heaven as others. People who obey God will live in heavenly houses made of valuable gold, silver, and jewels. People who disobey God and do wrong will live in houses made of cheap

Do you remember the children's story about the Three Little Pigs? One pig built his house out of straw, and the Big Bad Wolf blew it down. He blew down the house of sticks, too. But the house built out of bricks was so strong, he couldn't blow it down. That's the kind of house you want to build in Heaven.

sticks, hay, and straw (1 Corinthians 3:11–15).

When you live life, here on Earth, in a way that makes God proud of you, then you will have a big, strong house to live in when you get to Heaven.

Running for the Prize

Jesus' follower Paul had another way of looking at heavenly rewards. He described our life here on Earth as a race when we're running toward the finish line. Unlike an ordinary race, we aren't racing against other people. We're just trying to do "our personal best." Paul said:

Don't you realize that in a race everyone runs, but only one person gets the prize? So run to win! All athletes are disciplined in their training. They do it to win a prize that will fade away, but we do it for an eternal (forever) prize. 1 CORINTHIANS 9:24–25 NLT

Paul meant that we should do our very best to please God all the way through our life here on Earth. In races here on Earth, just one person wins. But in Heaven, everyone is a winner!

The prize that we receive at the end of our life on Earth is forever life in Heaven. This is promised to everyone who loves Jesus. That's why Paul said: "I press on to reach the end of the race and receive the heavenly prize" (Philippians 3:14 NLT).

The Judgment Seat of Christ

The Bible tells us that someday we'll need to explain to Jesus everything we have said and done here on Earth. That's why we should be careful what we do and say. Jesus said:

"You can be sure that on the Judgment Day you will have to give account of every useless word you have ever spoken." MATTHEW 12:36 GNT

And Paul tells us:

Remember, we will all stand before the judgment seat of God. . . . Yes, each of us will give a personal account to God. ROMANS 14:10, 12 NLT

The Judgment Seat of Christ is not to decide whether we go to Heaven. We were headed to Heaven the day we trusted Jesus to save us. This Judgment Seat is where we're rewarded for how we served Him—or receive consequences for not serving Him.

What does it mean to "give an account"? It means we'll have to explain the things we have done and said. Then we'll be rewarded for the good we've done. We will also have to accept the consequences for the wrong we've done—or for the good things we didn't do.

For we must all appear before the judgment seat of Christ, so that each of us may receive what is due us for the things done while in the body, whether good or bad. 2 CORINTHIANS 5:10 NIV

Think of the Judgment Seat like a family meeting with your mom or dad. If they told you to clean your room and you obeyed, you'll make them happy and earn a reward. But if you didn't obey, you might lose your video games for a week. You're still your parents' child, and they still love you—but because you disobeyed them, you lost a reward you could have had.

If you believe in Jesus, you'll go to Heaven. However, your choices in this life are still *very* important. What you do and what you say truly matters. That's why it's important to live right and to obey God.

The Crown of Life

Have you ever pretended that you are a king or queen wearing a crown? Well, you will get a real crown when you get to Heaven! It's called "the Crown of Life."

God blesses those who patiently endure testing and temptation. Afterward they will receive the crown of life that God has promised to those who love him.
JAMES 1:12 NLT

Some Christians imagine these crowns as heavy crowns with spikes, like kings and queens in storybooks wear. But the Crown of Life is more like

- a laurel wreath—a small circle made from an evergreen plant
- a "circlet"—a royal crown shaped like a thin, golden band

This Crown of Life is also called the Crown of Righteousness. And it's given to all true Christians.

And now the prize awaits me—the crown of righteousness, which the Lord, the righteous Judge, will give me on the day of his return. And the prize is not just for me but for all who eagerly look forward to his appearing.
2 TIMOTHY 4:8 NLT

In Revelation 6:2, the Greek word *stephanos* means a circlet, a golden band shaped something like a halo. This is where the idea came from that Christians wear halos in Heaven.

Every Christian will wear a Crown of Life. But very likely some people's crowns will glow with much more light than others. Probably the beauty and glory of our crown depends on how much we live our lives for Jesus Christ here on Earth. God will reward us for

- loving Him and other people
- praying for others
- reading and studying the Bible
- sharing our things with others
- helping people even when we don't feel like it
- being kind to difficult people
- being patient and not getting angry easily
- forgiving others and not trying to get even when someone hurts us

Crowns for Faithful Service

There are other kinds of crowns in Heaven, like the "Crown of Glory." Not all Christians get these special crowns. You earn these by serving God and living your life as a good example to other believers. Jesus' disciple Peter said—

Don't act as if you were a ruler over those who are under your care. Instead, be examples to the flock. The Chief Shepherd will come again. Then you will receive the crown of glory. It is a crown that will never fade away. 1 PETER 5:3–4 NIrV

You may wonder, "Can someone have more than *one* crown in Heaven?" Jesus does. Since He is the "King of kings," He has *many* crowns on His head (Revelation 19:12, 16).

In the Bible, King David wore the crown of the kingdom of Israel. But when he conquered another kingdom, he added that crown to his collection of crowns here on Earth. When he took over the kingdom of Ammon, he put their king's crown on his head (2 Samuel 12:29–30).

The Crown of Life (also called the Crown of Righteousness) is given to *all* believers—and it won't be taken away from them.

The Crown of Glory is a special reward for serving God. And yes, you can lose this crown by *not* doing what God called you to do. Jesus said:

"I am coming soon. Hold on to what you have, so that no one will take away your crown." REVELATION 3:11 NLT

If God has given you a job to do, and you refuse to do it, He will find someone else to do the work. And they'll receive the reward instead. Here are some ways to *not* lose your crown:

- be thankful for the job God has given you
- refuse to grumble and complain
- pray for patience and energy to keep going
- remind yourself how you're helping others
- remember that you'll be rewarded

What kind of jobs does God give to His people? The jobs are related to the "gifts" God gives us: "We have different gifts, according to the grace given to each of us. If your gift is prophesying, then prophesy in accordance with your faith; if it is serving, then serve; if it is teaching, then teach; if it is to encourage, then give encouragement; if it is giving, then give generously; if it is to lead, do it diligently; if it is to show mercy, do it cheerfully" (Romans 12:6–8 NIV).

Stars in Your Crown

Have you ever heard the expression, "stars in my crown"? Many Christians believe that if we help others to believe in Jesus, that our heavenly crown will have tiny, brilliant stars. Do people actually have crowns of stars? When John was in Heaven, he saw a vision of a woman:

And there appeared a great wonder in heaven; a woman clothed with the sun, and the moon under her feet, and upon her head a crown of twelve stars. REVELATION 12:1 KJV

And Paul said that the people he won to Jesus were his crown. He wrote:

I love you and long to see you, dear friends, for you are my joy and the crown I receive for my work. PHILIPPIANS 4:1 NLT

For sure God will reward us for winning others to trust in Jesus—and many Christians believe that we receive a gleaming star in our crown for every person we lead to Him. *Whatever* that "star" is, it will be wonderful!

In Heaven, we'll love God even more than the things He gives us. Even the twenty-four elders (very important men) sitting near God's throne take their crowns off and lay them down before God, every single time they worship Him (Revelation 4:10–11).

Great Rewards in Heaven

Jesus promises that we'll be rewarded for living in a way that pleases Him. For example, those who are made fun of because they stand up for Jesus will be rewarded greatly:

Happy are you when people hate you, reject you, insult you, and say that you are evil, all because of the Son of Man! Be glad when that happens. . .because a great reward is kept for you in heaven. Luke 6:22–23 GNT

We'll also be rewarded for obeying Jesus' commands. He told us to love our enemies and to do good even to unthankful people. Sometimes that's not easy to do, but those who love even their enemies will receive rewards from God.

"Love your enemies! Do good to them. Lend to them without expecting to be repaid. Then your reward from heaven will be very great." Luke 6:35 NLT

Chapter 7
Why Does Heaven Have to Wait?

Going to Heaven

Right now, the only people in Heaven are Christians who have died. When they left their human bodies, God sent His angels to come take them to Heaven. Jesus talked about this when He described what happened when a man named Lazarus died:

"The time came when the beggar died. The angels carried him to Abraham's side" (to Heaven). LUKE 16:22 NIrV

We miss our loved ones who are in Heaven. We wish we could go to Heaven for a short visit, to see them. But this is almost impossible when we have our human bodies. We have to die—or almost die—to go to Heaven. Sometimes, but not often, God allows a human a short look inside, as He did John and Paul.

God took John to Heaven, and then John wrote the book of Revelation to tell us what he'd seen and heard there (Revelation 4:1–2). Paul went to Heaven for a visit, but he didn't say what he saw. He heard some amazing things, but he wasn't allowed to share them (2 Corinthians 12:2–4).

Even John wasn't allowed to tell us everything. One time, he heard an angel shouting. Then seven thunders answered with a roar. John was going to write about it, but a voice said, "Keep secret what the seven thunders have said; do not write it down!" (Revelation 10:4 GNT).

The Rapture and Resurrection

Right now, Heaven has to wait until we die. But the good news is this: *All* Christians are going to Heaven someday—and millions won't have to die and leave their human bodies first. Jesus is coming back to Earth someday, and when He does, He will send out His angels to gather people all at the same time from all over the Earth. This special event is called "the Rapture," and no one knows when it will happen.

> *"And they will see the Son of Man coming on the clouds of heaven with power and great glory. And he will send out his angels with the mighty blast of a trumpet, and they will gather his chosen ones from all over the world."*
> MATTHEW 24:30–31 NLT

Here's what will happen when Jesus returns from Heaven:

- He will appear in the clouds of the sky
- the people who live in Heaven will come with Him
- their human bodies will be raised from the dead and become heavenly, forever bodies
- these forever bodies will rise up and become one with their spirits
- then everyone who is still living on Earth will get new, perfect, forever bodies, too
- their changed bodies will rise up to Jesus
- every Christian—those who have already died and those who are still living on Earth—will go to Heaven together

Today when Christians die, they leave their human bodies behind. They no longer have human bodies. But God doesn't want them to be that way forever. Just as He resurrected (brought back to life) the body of His Son, Jesus, He will bring back to life their human bodies, too.

If the Spirit of God, who raised Jesus from death, lives in you, then he who raised Christ from death will also give life to your mortal bodies. ROMANS 8:11 GNT

To be *resurrected* means to be "raised from the dead." Our weak human bodies die. But one day God will bring them back to life. They will become perfect, supernatural, and forever bodies. These are called our "resurrection bodies."

Some people think that Christians get their final forever bodies as soon as they go to Heaven. This isn't so. Human bodies coming alive again happens when Jesus returns—and He hasn't returned yet. People who have already died will come back with Jesus someday, and their human bodies will rise from the Earth. Then *fwoosh*! Their spirits will enter their new, perfect human bodies.

The Lord himself will come down from heaven. We will hear a loud command. We will hear the voice of the leader of the angels. We will hear a blast from God's trumpet. Many who believe in Christ will have died already. They will rise first. After that, we who are still alive and are left will be caught up together with them. We will be taken up in the clouds. We will meet the Lord in the air. And we will be with him forever. 1Thessalonians 4:16–17 NIrV

The Rapture is when those who are alive here on Earth when Jesus comes back are "caught up" by the angels. They will carry the Christians on Earth to be with Jesus and everyone in Heaven. The word *rapture* comes from the Latin word *raptus*—which means to "carry off."

It doesn't matter whether people are living on Earth or in Heaven on rapture day. Everyone who believes in Jesus will be changed and given brand-new perfect bodies.

We shall not all die, but when the last trumpet sounds, we shall all be changed in an instant, as quickly as the blinking of an eye. For when the trumpet sounds, the dead will be raised, never to die again, and we shall all be changed.
1 CORINTHIANS 15:51–52 GNT

If you wonder why Christians have to wait to receive our forever bodies, this is why: we have to wait for Jesus to return and give them to us. Jesus says in the book of Revelation, "I am coming soon!" The apostle John wrote, "Amen! Come, Lord Jesus!" (Revelation 22:20 NLT).

Our Resurrection Body

Our bodies are human bodies right now. They're weak and they grow old and die. But one day they'll be glorious bodies. Paul explained:

When you plant something, it isn't a completely grown plant that you put in the ground. You only plant a seed . . . . It will be like that with bodies that are raised from the dead. 1 CORINTHIANS 15:37, 42 NIrV

Your forever body is so, so much better and more glorious than your earthly body. Think of it this way: a caterpillar is not so pretty. It is not so glorious. It can only crawl along slowly on a branch. But after the caterpillar sleeps for a while in a cocoon, it goes through an amazing change! When it comes out it is a glorious and beautiful butterfly! It can fly in the sky! That is how much better your forever body will be than the body you have now!

Our physical bodies will be changed—just like Jesus' body was! One day we will be transformed and receive beautiful, powerful, amazing forever bodies! What will our new bodies look like? Let's see!

Our final, forever bodies will be "transformed." That means they will be changed, and changed into something perfectly wonderful. Jesus was transformed for a moment when He talked with our Bible friends Moses and Elijah up on a mountain (Matthew 17:1–3). After Jesus rose from the dead, His body was transformed forever!

When a caterpillar becomes a butterfly, we call the change a "metamorphosis." The forever bodies of God's people will be even more beautiful.

Faces Glowing Like the Sun

When He stood on a mountain and spoke with Moses and Elijah, Jesus' appearance was transformed so that His face shone like the sun, and His clothes became as white as light (Matthew 17:2).

When John saw Jesus years later in Heaven (Revelation 1:14–16 NIV), he described Jesus this way:

- The hair on his head was white like wool, as white as snow.
- His eyes were like blazing fire.
- His feet were like bronze glowing in a furnace.
- His face was like the sun shining in all its brilliance.

John tells us, "But we know that when Christ appears, we shall be like him" (1 John 3:2 NIV). Jesus' face had a bright, sunny glow, and so will ours—though not as bright.

Then shall the righteous shine forth as the sun in the kingdom of their Father.
MATTHEW 13:43 KJV

After spending forty days and nights with God, His follower Moses' face and skin glowed with the glory of the Lord (Exodus 34:28–30). This may happen to us when we get our resurrection bodies. God's Spirit may cause us to glow.

Different Like the Stars

An angel told Daniel:

"Those who are wise will shine like the brightness of the heavens, and those who lead many to righteousness, like the stars for ever and ever." DANIEL 12:3 NIV

Just like every star in the universe is different, our new bodies will glow with different amounts of brightness.

There is one glory of the sun, another glory of the moon, and another glory of the stars; for one star differs from another star in glory. 1 CORINTHIANS 15:41 NKJV

There are many different stars in the universe. Some are large and bright; others are small and dim. For example, red supergiants are thousands of times bigger than white dwarfs. Here are some stars:

- yellow stars (like our sun)
- red giants
- red supergiants
- blue supergiants
- white dwarfs
- brown dwarfs
- neutron stars

Maybe part of our reward in Heaven is that the closer we are to God on Earth, and the more we spend time in His presence, the more His brightness comes into our life. Then in Heaven, we will shine like the stars forever.

The Millennium (One Thousand Years)

Certain things must happen before Jesus comes back to Earth. People who love Jesus will get their new, perfect bodies. Then a big war called the Battle of Armageddon will happen. Evil, wicked nations will make war against Jesus. But Jesus and all His Christian friends will return from Heaven and win that war. Then Jesus will reign as the Great King over all the Earth, and Christians will reign along with Him, for one thousand years.

Blessed and holy are those who share in the first resurrection. . .they will be priests of God and of Christ and will reign with him for a thousand years. REVELATION 20:6 NIV

There will be no more war, or hunger, or poor people. Jesus will rule the Earth as a good and perfect King. He will show the world what a truly good government is like. It will be wonderful. But things won't be perfect yet, because many people living on Earth will still be against Jesus. They'll still want to live selfishly. That's why Jesus will have to be firm with them, like your parents are with you when they tell you "no."

Our English word *millennium* comes
from two Latin words, *mille* (thousand)
and *ennium* (years). The Earth will be spoiled
by pollution and the Battle of Armageddon,
but one day, Jesus will clean it up and make it
a Paradise for a thousand years.

"To all who are victorious, who obey me to the very end, to them I will give authority over all the nations. They will rule the nations with an iron rod." Revelation 2:26–27 NLT

The New Jerusalem—Heaven on Earth

Right now the heavenly city, New Jerusalem, is in the heavenly dimension where only people who have died can live. But one day that city is going to come down and sit on the Earth. Here's how it will happen:

At the end of the thousand years, although Jesus has ruled perfectly, the selfish people living on the Earth will turn against Him. They'll rise up to make war against Jesus. That's when God will destroy the Earth as we know it (2 Peter 3:10). All the bad people will finally be gone.

Then I saw a new heaven and a new earth, for the old heaven and the old earth had disappeared. And the sea was also gone. Revelation 21:1 NLT

Right now, water covers most of our planet. But when God destroys the Earth, the oceans will be gone. Earth will

- have lots of land for everyone to live on
- have many large lakes, and ponds, and rivers to enjoy
- be transformed into a Paradise, like the Garden of Eden
- have a new atmosphere

- have perfect weather all the time
- have no more sickness or other bad things
- be filled with beautiful, tame animals

And the best part is that once the entire world has become a gigantic Garden of Eden, God Himself will come to live here forever. Wow! Can you imagine that?

I saw the Holy City, the new Jerusalem. It was coming down out of heaven. . . . I heard a loud voice from the throne. It said, "Now God makes his home with people. He will live with them. They will be his people. And God himself will be with them and be their God." Revelation 21:2–3 NIrV

Some people call Hawaii a "paradise," like the Garden of Eden. But God's new earth will be even better than the best spot on earth today.

Not only will the heavenly city be on Earth but the entire new planet Earth will be a perfect Garden of Eden. It will be even better than it was when Jesus ruled it as King. It will truly be "Heaven on Earth." And if you believe in Jesus and love Him, that's where you'll be!

Questions to Think About

What do you think it'll be like standing before the throne of God? Do you think you'll be scared or will you be totally amazed?

The Bible says that "God is love" (1 John 4:8). How much love do you think you'll feel when God looks at you? A little, or a lot, or a huge amount?

Jesus said, "Those who are victorious will sit with me on my throne" (Revelation 3:21 NLT). What do you think it will be like sitting with Jesus on His throne?

Who is the first person you would like to see in Heaven? What would you want to ask him or her?

What Bible person would you want to sit down and talk with? What kinds of questions would you ask him or her?

What do you imagine your heavenly home will look like? What will your garden be like? Who do you want living with you—or right beside you?

If you could choose animals to live in your heavenly garden, which ones would you choose?

There will be no more tears or sadness in Heaven. What do you think it'll be like to be peaceful and happy all the time? Do you think you'll laugh a lot in Heaven?

Heaven is full of exciting, fantastic, interesting things to do! What are some things that you'd really enjoy doing in Heaven?

Do you think you'll be able to fly like a bird in Heaven? If so, will you soar like Superman high above the hills and rivers and people below?

In Paradise there'll be "waters to swim in" (Ezekiel 47:5 KJV). Will you enjoy swimming with Heaven's sea turtles? How long do you think you'll be able to hold your breath with your new body?

What kind of jobs would you enjoy doing in Heaven?

What kind of things would you enjoy learning about? Which places would you like to explore?

What do you think heavenly food will taste like? What do you think the fruit of the Tree of Life will taste like?

Now that you know you'll be rewarded in Heaven for the good you do on Earth, does it help you want to obey God? What good things can you do to please God?

Have you asked God to help you to "love your enemies"? Do you pray for those who are unkind to you?

Are you sure that you'll go to Heaven one day? Have you prayed and asked Jesus to forgive your sins and come into your life?